SIMPLE TRUTH

SIMPLE TRUTH

Ideas and Experiences
for Humans from
Less-Than-Perfect Families

Thom Rutledge

By the same author:

IF I WERE THEY: A Handbook of Practical Recovery Wisdom

PRACTICE MAKES PRACTICE: From Self-Judgment to Self-Compassion

For a free catalog from Thom Rutledge Publishing, write or call:

331 22nd Avenue North
Suite One
Nashville, Tennessee 37203
(615) 327-3423

Copyright © 1990 by Thom Rutledge
ISBN: 0-962-7963-0-1
Second Printing 1994

Cover design by Leslie Wilson and Doris Estes
Illustrations by Karensky
Printed by Vaughan Printing, Nashville, Tennessee

For One Loving Spirit:
Dede and Annie

ACKNOWLEDGEMENTS

Thank you first to Dede Beasley for creating with me this loving and honest relationship in which I can feel safe enough to go to my room and write.

Thank you to Trish Sanders, my friend and spirit-sister, for listening to every word I wrote and providing the irreplaceable service of fending off my harsh inner-critic.

Thank you to all the teachers, therapists and guides who helped me to reclaim my life — especially to Bedford Combs, Judy Johnson, Linda Odom, Hillary Ellers and Serenity Peterson.

Thank you to my friends for reading this manuscript and talking to me about it — and to Dan Mason for being ahead of me on the writing path and allowing me to benefit from his experience.

I could not have written what follows without the clients who have trusted themselves and me enough to participate in the ongoing experiment of psychotherapy. Thanks to *each* of them.

Thank you to Bedford and Kristy Combs for the professional opportunity to grow "beyond my wildest dreams" and most of all for being buds.

Thank you to Elizabeth Ann Browning of Plainview, Texas for inspiring an adolescent to write. And thank you to my parents for always encouraging my creative self: when I was going to be a famous magician, you never laughed . . . I think you believed me.

Thank you to Peg Price-Hurt and Betsy Carlisle and their magic machines. And thanks to Betsy, the emerging editor. Thanks to Doris Estes for making the book cover simple, to Karensky Miller for the wonderful illustrations, to Stuart, Doreen, and Marlene of TOTAL CONCEPTS, INC. for their competence, hard work *and* their sense of humor.

Last but not least: A great big hug and kiss for Silven, Doc and Writer, the best friends a boy could have.

CONTENTS

INTRODUCTION

I have never considered my approach to the work of psychotherapy, and now my approach to writing this book, particularly clinical. The process called psychotherapy is a collaboration, an experience of teaching and learning *shared* by two or more individuals in an atmosphere of unconditional emotional safety. At this point in my life and in my career I am realizing that I have earned veteran status on both sides of this collaboration (as therapist and as client). It is from this experience of collaboration that I offer this book called *Simple Truth*, so named because I believe that all truth is simple. It seems inherent to our human condition that we make the work of getting to simplicity such a complex task.

In an effort to remain separate from *my addiction* to complexity, I practice tuning in to my intuition — my receiving station for Higher Power wisdom and direction — one day at a time. From this place of intuition, I teach what occurs to me to teach. I learn what I am ready and willing to learn. And I am willing to make mistakes in this process of teaching and learning. As nearly as I can tell, making mistakes is one very important and effective way that I learn.

What follows are some of life's lessons that have occurred to me over the past several years. The context for these lessons has as often been my personal life as it has been my work as a psychotherapist and workshop facilitator. Most often, the application is simultaneous.

1

As the title suggests, the format for this book is simple. I want it to be useful to you. Some of the entries may seem self-contained — to be read, thought about for a moment and then let go. I hope that some of the entries will bump into you a bit — or help you to reach inside to explore something new . . . or perhaps something old and stuck.

I have written each entry as independently as possible from the other material in the book so that there is no particular order for reading *Simple Truth*. The exceptions to this are three entries toward the center of the book ("Family Lessons","Should-Monster","A New Identity") that I perceive as a trilogy to be read in that order. Still, not even that is necessary. Read what is of interest. Use what is helpful.

When I read books that ask me to stop before proceeding and do an exercise, I usually read right on through. "No author can tell me what to do!" my rebellious side mumbles. So it seems ironic that I write a book full of exercises — exercises that I hope you will work with "before proceeding."

Don't get me wrong. I do not imagine that every suggested experience included here will be helpful for every potential reader out there. I simply suggest that to maximize the benefit of this book, go slow. *Use* this book as you read it.

And finally, whenever possible I hope that you will work with this book in groups. The power that comes from loving, supportive, safe group work is like no other. To openly share your true inner-self with others may well be experienced as a much greater risk than a one to one relationship or a one person to one book relationship; but, the pay-off for taking such a risk is infinitely greater.

So within these pages my wish for you is that you learn what you are ready and willing to learn, and that you teach yourself and others what occurs to you to teach. *And* that you be willing to do the important work of mistake-making.

TO PROFESSIONAL PEOPLE-HELPERS

Thanks for buying my book. I hope that you will *experience yourself* in these ideas and exercises before delivering this material to your clients, patients, and students. The first step to giving is always receiving.

And then, I hope you will find *Simple Truth* helpful in your work.

Experiment. Follow your intuition. Improvise. And let me know what happens.

A NOTE ABOUT "RECOVERY"

Throughout this book I use the word "recovery" to refer to a new path taken by those of us who have become dissatisfied enough with our old *circular* paths to venture out, risking the letting go of old ways and experimenting with new.

The word "recovery" has become a natural part of my vocabulary as a "recovering" alcoholic and codependent person. But the word has come to mean much more to me than a simple reminder of where I have been (alcoholism, dysfunctional and irresponsible relationships). It speaks to me of where I am bound.

It is not enough for me to hold my focus on these conditions and behaviors I am recovering *from*. The miracle of the new paths I have taken, and continue to take one day at a time, is found in what I am in the process of discovering of myself — literally the me that I am *recovering* (meaning regaining).

It is not necessary that you share with me the identification of alcoholism or codependency in order to identify with this generic use of the word "recovery". Herein, "recovery" simply means *possessing the courage to let go of old ineffective patterns of thought and behavior and a willingness to start fresh.*

Before we are one,
we are many.

A NEW DEFINITION
FOR SANITY

One fool-proof method for driving ourselves crazy is to attempt to be singular in nature: To have *one* opinion or *one* feeling about something or someone. Knowing this *one* thought and/or this *one* emotion, I call myself sane.

"Then why do I feel so crazy!"

We simply will not fit into such small packages. As growing, recovering human beings, this erroneous definition for sanity (that we are singular in nature) begins to cause more discomfort than comfort. We feel confined, as in fact we are. We need room to expand. We need appreciation for our depth, for the *expanded* version of ourselves. We need to honor the "all" of who we are without the endless inner-censorship of "either-or" mentality:

"Do I feel this way or that?"
"Either I think this or I think that."
"I must make up my mind."
"I don't know what I truly feel."
"I must be nuts!"
"First I feel one way, and then another."
"I've got to get a grip."

It is not easy to so radically change our definition for sanity, but that is what is called for here. A teacher of mine once startled me into this new definition by writing this note to me:

"The answer to all 'either-or' questions is . . . yes."

Of course, I responded inwardly wondering, "Can this be true *or* is it not?" Of course. Of course.

Just as we live in one world made up of many continents divided into many countries containing many states and provinces, consisting of communities within communities within communities, we are also each one person containing many parts (or sub-personalities). In fact, we are each made up of quite a variety of these unique personalities, personalities who stand a much better chance of living harmoniously within us once we let go of the belief that every one of them is supposed to think and feel alike.

I have yet to teach this concept to anyone who could not identify with it, and yet as a society and as families we persist in treating each other and ourselves as if we are supposed to walk around in some sort of singular, unanimous inner-agreement. Otherwise we call ourselves *confused* (at best) and *insane* (at worst).

I am many. You are many. This is the beginning for a new definition of sanity. With this exercise expand your awareness of your own "multiple-nature", and for the time being simply acknowledge the presence of more than one you.

Sounds a little crazy. Can be fun.

EXERCISE

As with all of the exercises to follow, there is no wrong way to do this. I will offer the guidelines and then whatever you experience is to be valued. When you feel inwardly guided to alter or expand on an exercise, by all means do so. This book is intended as a catalyst for your growth. Please never allow it to confine you.

Whenever possible share your experience with someone you trust.

You will need a pen and paper or markers/crayons and art paper. Sit quietly for a few minutes, inviting your imagination and/or your spiritual guidance to join you. Consider that there are several personalities within the one you.

Become an observer of these personalities, granting yourself enough distance to avoid becoming trapped in any one of them. Choose one or two of the more prominent, well defined personalities of which you become aware, and focus your attention on each of them — one at a time.

Of the inner-personalities you have chosen, notice the various characteristics of each. In your mind try becoming one personality and then the other. Or it may feel safer to continue experiencing them from the "outside" as an observer.

What does each personality look or feel like physically? Is there tension or relaxation? How does each seem or feel emotionally: Scared? Angry? Happy? Shameful? And how does each personality think: Cynical and distrusting? Blaming and vengeful? Naive? Trusting and positive? And what specifically does each personality think and feel about you? Is one in direct conflict with another? Does one personality seem to be supportive, while another attacks? And on and on. Trust your imagination.

After you have experienced enough to feel in touch with the more-than-one-you, use your writing and drawing material to depict your experience. Write descriptive words to characterize each personality and/or draw pictures of them or of their relationships with one another. If you are working in a group or with a partner, remain non-verbal until you complete your depiction. Then share what you have discovered.

And finally, if this experience has left you with some unanswered questions, write the questions down and then close the exercise. It may be tough to walk away with unanswered questions, but that is what I am suggesting that you do. And I am suggesting that you call *all* of this, including your unanswered questions, SANITY.

Important note:

As we expand with the power of our awareness, and as we learn to resist the temptation to deny our multiple-nature, we will experience a new kind of discomfort and even pain. Call this "growing pain."

JIG SAW PUZZLE

Awareness is putting all the pieces on the table and turning them face up.
Healing is the gradual process of putting the pieces together.
Insight is seeing the picture take form.

Healing is preceded by Awareness and followed by Insight.

Again: Insight follows healing. Not vice versa. All too often we block emotional healing with a deeply embedded cultural belief that we must first fully "understand" before we can transform.

NOT SO. FIRST THINGS FIRST.

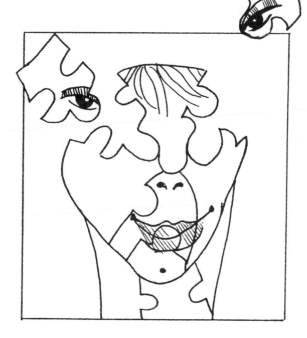

The answer
to the question,
"When am I going to learn?"
is...

"always."

INCREASING TOLERANCE

Essential to becoming an alcoholic is an increased tolerance for alcohol. Without this important early symptom I would not have stood a fair chance at developing my alcoholism.

To increase that tolerance all I needed was three ingredients: 1) The *capability* or potential for physical tolerance (genetic brain chemistry), 2) The *availability* of alcohol (no problem), and 3) The *motivation/dedication* to ingest that alcohol on a regular basis. (Again, no problem.) Then, all that was left to do was take pride in being able to "hold my liquor."

Many of us — alcoholics and non-alcoholics — grow up in our less-than-perfect families with another version of increased tolerance: *A high tolerance for emotional pain.* Sometimes our tolerance for pain is so high that we do not even recognize the feelings we experience as painful. And even when we do, we inwardly "take pride" in our tolerance, regarding this ability to ignore our emotions as a show of strength. To further complicate matters, we live in a society that tends to support this definition for strength.

Accompanying high pain tolerance is low "pleasure tolerance". This is actually an intolerance for receiving pleasure (positive affirmation), especially when it is offered unconditionally. Ironically, this means that supportive, loving conditions may be experienced as far more painful than remaining stuck in old, ineffective patterns of living. Very simply: When we begin to invite those supportive, loving conditions into our lives . . . it hurts.

In recovery, as we take responsibility for our own lives and let go of thinking ourselves responsible for everyone else, pain tolerance begins a descent. This happens quite naturally when we begin to recognize our own value. At this stage we become increasingly aware of old pain we have long hidden, as well as the pain we experience in our present daily lives.

Positive though this is, many of us, habituated to pain, are tempted to remain with this new pain-focus around the clock, leaving our low "pleasure-tolerance" helpless and atrophied.

It is an important goal of recovery to bring these two into balance — decreasing the pain tolerance *and* increasing the pleasure-tolerance.

EXERCISE

Sit quietly for a few minutes considering what you already know about your own low pleasure-tolerance. Specifically identify characteristic ways that you block positive affirmation from others. Examples of these defensive blocks include laughing off compliments or kind statements directed to you, changing the subject, explaining away compliments, immediately giving credit to others, avoiding eye contact, etc. Inwardly, we defend against positive regard from others by telling ourselves we do not deserve what we are hearing, or by discounting the person offering the affirmation, telling ourselves that if that person really knew us, he/she would no longer say such positive things. Most blatantly, some of us will completely "tune-out" anyone offering unconditional, loving support.

By taking this honest inner-inventory you will reduce the effectiveness of your characteristic defenses for the remainder of this exercise. You may even choose to make a commitment to yourself *not* to use these defenses until the exercise is complete.

Now, here is the first challenge to your pleasure-tolerance: *Make a list of the most gentle, compassionate messages to yourself that you are willing to imagine.*

Stretch that tolerance. Write whatever comes to mind, including specific statements about *what you do* and have done, and broader statements about *who you are*, and who you are becoming. It is not necessary that you believe everything that you write. It is only necessary that you be willing to write the positive messages down. Try writing at least ten of these messages. Write each message as if it is true now and precede each with your name.

i.e.   Thom, you are a kind and loving man.
       Thom, I love you no matter what.
       Thom, it is important for you to make mistakes.
       Thom, you are a good writer.
       Thom, you are free to do as you please.
       Thom, I will always be here for you.
       Thom, you did an excellent job in group therapy
            yesterday.
       Thom, you are a good friend.

If you want to take this a step farther, have someone you trust sit with you in a comfortable, quiet place and read your messages to you. Your mission, should you decide to accept it, will be the sometimes difficult task of remaining non-verbal (so as not to block the messages), breathing gently and absorbing the loving support in your messages.

Remember: If it hurts, that is growing pain. But be careful not to overwork the atrophied pleasure-tolerance. Be gentle and stop when you need to. After all, taking excellent care of yourself is what this is all about.

Keep your list of compassionate messages. Go back to them everyday for the next week to ten days, and read them aloud to yourself. Read them and receive them into your heart. Feel whatever you need to feel in response. And add new messages as your tolerance increases.

To achieve the essential increased tolerance for my alcoholism all I needed was three ingredients. The same three ingredients are also all that are needed to increase your pleasure tolerance:

1)   The *capability or potential* for tolerance.
     (This exists in the deepest part of our spirit.)

2)   The *availability* of loving support.
     (It is our responsibility to discover where this "drink" is served.)

3)   The *motivation/dedication* to "ingest" that loving support on a regular basis.

As Alcoholic's Anonymous puts it, "Keep coming back ... It works."

A CHANCE FOR PEACE

When we let go of the constant attempts to solve the "content" of our lives, and

Attend to the important "process" of how we treat ourselves and each other,

We have a real chance for peace.

FRIEND

Know this: When you turn inward to connect and converse with the intuitive, wisest part of you —your inner-teacher — or when you (in meditation) stretch to reach the highest level of consciousness humanly imaginable, you are not attempting to contact a foreigner within you or some outer space being. You are sitting down to talk with your oldest and dearest friend. Trust this connection. It is eternal.

ADOLESCENT-WITHIN

My relationship with the
 adolescent within me:

I love him. He hates himself.

*I can feel **both**.*

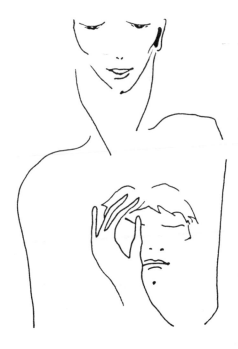

DIVINE EMPTINESS

"I don't know."

A frightening concept. A living hell. And a blank space to be filled at once — no questions asked . . . just fill 'er up with some "known". I sure as hell can't live with "I don't know."

Many of us have expertly survived growing up in the midst of uncertainty and unpredictability by convincing ourselves that we "know", that we understand what is happening around us, inside us, and that we "know" exactly what to do about it. To protect this delusional state of mind, we have had to don reality blinders, consequently limiting the view of our own potential.

If this rings true for you, then *know* this: *It has not felt safe* for you to simply say "I...don't...know."

As we approach and proceed with the self examination of recovery, we soon tread on this treacherous ground of wide open uncertainty. As our willingness to become completely honest with self and loved ones expands, so does the awareness of our own personal "I don't know-ness".

This previously avoided territory will likely access feelings of inadequacy, weakness and unworthiness. And, when we feel these fears in the center of the empty "I don't know-ness" . . . we can stand proud for we are making excellent progress.

This may sound strange, backwards and certainly against the grain of existing mental programming, but consider this:

It is at this very point where we have time and again, consciously and unconsciously, turned back in our previous attempts to change. It is this emptiness that has so frightened us that we automatically have returned to old, ineffective patterns of living and relating.

So how would it be different if we could feel safe enough to take the plunge — to dive head long into the pool of "permission-to-not-know-anything?"

EXERCISE

Another bit of wisdom commonly heard in and around Alcoholics Anonymous is this: "It's simple, but not easy." I believe that slogan applies well to this exercise.

As with the other experiences, sit quietly to begin, focusing inward. Making contact with your inner-self or Higher Power, invite the awareness of all of your uncertainty to come to your center and to expand. Open yourself to all that you do not know. Become aware of your total response to this suggestion: What do you think, feel and experience physically when you openly invite your "I don't know-ness" to enter —and even to expand?

Witness whatever resistance is present, and remain willing to feel whatever fear arises. As always, trust your imagination and your inner-guidance. Stay with whatever you experience for a few minutes.

Next: Write down a list of "I don't know's." Move past as much inner-censorship as possible, writing as quickly as the phrases come to your mind.

I don't know why...
I don't know what...
I don't know how...
I don't know if...

Whatever you write is fine. Just begin each phrase with "I don't know" and at the end of your list write the following words in as large of print as you are willing:

"AND I DON'T HAVE TO KNOW!"

If you are using this exercise in a group setting you may choose next to pair off to share your lists, or simply to take turns reading your "I don't know's" to the group.

In a group also try this: After each person reads his/her list and finishes with an enthusiastic, "And I don't have to know!", the group responds in unison (loud and supportive), "No, person's name , you don't have to know!"

DIVINE EMPTINESS

When we let go of what we thought we knew and admit that "I don't know," a space is revealed inside of us; a space that until now has been avoided or filled at all costs.

Now we are ready to face our fears and leave the space open for a time. Call this space "Divine Emptiness". When so respected, the emptiness itself will attract what we now need. Admitting that we do not know, we become quite teachable. Remaining this open is frightening, but not impossible.

And how do you know if the emptiness you are feeling is divine? A friend of mine says, "You know that it's *Divine* Emptiness if it scares the *hell* out of you."

SAFETY AND FEAR

*Being safe and feeling fear are not opposites.
One of the great challenges of recovery is finding our
way to feel safe enough to finally experience our
deepest fears.*

Safe...Scared...Then...Free!

Amen

BOREDOM AND PEACE

*The difference between boredom and being at peace
is the degree of comfort we have in our own company.*

INSTANT THERAPY

*I don't know how
to solve your problems.
I don't have to know.*

You don't have to know either.

That takes care of that problem.

Next........

WANT POWER

"I deserve everything that I want." Say that several times to yourself, slow and easy, and see what happens. Does it feel good? Do you begin to feel excited about all of life's treasures that will soon be coming your way? If so, that's wonderful. Keep saying it over and over and over.

For many of us, however, this grand statement of deservingness is first experienced as ridiculous and/or dangerous. Our bodies tense. Our vocal chords may even rebel, refusing to pronounce the sentence aloud. Fear and shame churn. And the objections rush into our brains.

Try it. Repeat the sentence aloud: "I deserve everything that I want." Turn your awareness inward. See, hear and feel your inner-responses. Write the responses down, *especially the objections.* In this way you are the master of your computer-brain, accessing negative programming that is getting in your way. Write it all down so that you can see it in front of you. You are Gary Cooper, refusing to be ambushed — calling your opponent into the street.

Your objections to deserving everything that you want will be your own unique objections, but it seems that for many of us they fall into two primary categories: "I don't have any idea what I really want" and "I cannot be trusted with that kind of power."

"I don't have any idea what I really want" is the understandable result of having lived a life necessarily focused on mental, emotional and sometimes physical *survival.* When has there been time (or permission) in such a life to consider

29

what we want? "Want" is a luxury reserved for others . . . for those mysterious "normal" people.

"I cannot be trusted with that kind of power" directly results from our being told or treated as if we can't be trusted. This objection implies that what we will want will exclude the greatest good for others — a sort of criminal mentality. If you are a criminal, please skip the next paragraph.

We are not criminals. And our receiving what we want does not have to deprive others of what they want *and* deserve. And we all deserve the time and permission (from self) to stop long enough to consider what we really want in our lives. What I want is an essential part of my core, of who I am.

EXERCISE

Please do not wait around to be convinced of your de-servingness before proceeding with this exercise. Try what follows as positive affirmation and/or a means of increasing awareness of your inner-obstacles to having what you want.

Another list: Write a series of "I want" statements.

> *I want* a healthy, happy relationship.
> *I want* to make a comfortable living
>   or
> *I want* to make XXX dollars per year.
> *I want* to publish this book.
> *I want* a trustworthy friend who understands me.
> *I want* to be free.
> *I want* to ride a roller coaster.
> *I want* a tangible contact with God.
> *I want* physical health.

Trust your intuition to communicate your "wants" to you. Step around the inner-censor.

Now, review your list, perhaps reading it aloud or even reading it to a friend (or group participant if you are working with this in a group.) As you read, if strong objections arise in you, write the objections down on a separate sheet of paper.

> I don't deserve a friend.
> If I had more money, I'd just waste it.
> This is a stupid exercise.
> There's no such thing as God.
> etc.

Next, rewrite your "want" list beginning each with the phrase "I deserve."

> *I deserve* a healthy, happy relationship.
> *I deserve* XXX dollars per year.
> etc.

Again, read what you have written aloud, and if objections arise write them on your separate objection page. If some of the same objections surface more than once, write them again. Be willing to see exactly what you are up against including the power of repetition.

Having done this, once again rewrite your original list using the phrase "I am ready for . . ."

> *I am ready* for a healthy, happy relationship.
> etc.

Review the list aloud a final time and make notes of objections as before.

For the next week, keep your "I want's", "I deserve's", "I am ready for's" in a safe place in your home. Keep your objection page in a separate place. On some of the days carry your "I want's, deserve's and ready for's" with you everywhere you go. Refer to them often or just remind yourself that they are in your pocket, purse or whatever. (Be sure to keep them close to you.)

On at least two or three days of the week, leave your positive messages at home in their safe place and carry your objection page with you. Carry them close and remember them.

Feel the difference. At the end of the week (in next week's group session if you are working with this in group) sit again with both lists. Read them aloud again, and then *decide what you want* to do with each list.

CLARIFICATIONS
OF "WANT-POWER"

- 1 -

*There is never anything wrong with **what I want**. I will, however, run into difficulties with how I go about obtaining what I want. For example: There is absolutely nothing wrong with my wanting a relaxed peace of mind, but there have been problems with my attempts to achieve this goal with alcohol. Also, there is nothing wrong with my wanting to feel accepted, but I have experienced great difficulty when I have decided that in order to be accepted I had to have a particular person's approval or acceptance.*

- 2 -

*Knowing what I want, affirming my deservingness and becoming ready to receive is **not** the same as **demanding** what I want.*

My experience teaches this: When I become ready, the timing is in God's hands.

DISSATISFACTION

Dissatisfaction is like gasoline.....

When we put it in our tanks, it becomes essential
fuel that will take us where we want to go.

When we sit around "huffing" it, it will destroy
our brains!

There is an important distinction to be made between
dissatisfaction, the fuel source
and
dissatisfaction, the intoxicant.

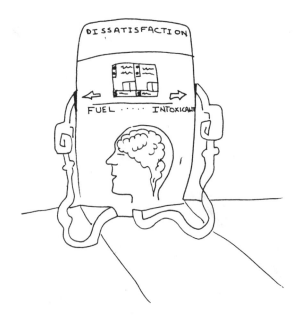

THE RISK OF WANTING

Once in touch with our pain, we have an important choice available to us:

Do I continue to live my life by default . . . or am I willing to risk wanting my life to be different?"

SIMPLE TRUTH

God can be mean. God can be unfeeling and cruel. Certainly God is rigid. Or so it seemed to me years ago when I first began to really pay attention to my clients' Gods. I noticed that some of my clients with a rigid God walked around in constant anxiety. When their lives were chaotic this feeling escalated into a dark cloud of dread. When all was well (or improving) in their lives, the anxiety just went into hiding, out of daily conscious awareness, but always present and frequently returning. God was not going to let them off the hook.

Other clients, with the unfeeling and cruel brand of God, were simply terrified. Apparently, there was little to nothing they could ever do to make up for what they had done up until now — and most curiously, many of them were not exactly sure what they had done that was so horrible. Of course others had long inventories of specific reasons for which they would surely burn.

Others of us are quite familiar with these same haunting feelings of fear and shame, and just don't happen to attribute them to God's judgement. We need no God to pass judgement on us; we can do it perfectly well ourselves, thank you.

So there I was noticing my clients' Gods when all of a sudden (a divine inspiration?) I thought:

"Wait a minute. I am a really nice guy. I haven't always been — certainly not all of the time. But as I progress in my recovery, as I continue to reach out for help when I need it, and as I hold fast to my commitment to being totally responsible for my own life, I have become a nice guy. I am a much better friend than I used to be. And as a therapist I sit here several days every week and listen attentively to people's stories. In response I feel compassion, understanding and even forgiveness. I seldom find myself caught up in what they have done. What I tend to notice — and connect with most — is *who they are*. And no matter what the story line, it is not difficult for me to see that these people are doing the best they know how. However misdirected their efforts may have been, their intentions come straight from the heart. 'The best they know how' is no longer working for them, and that is what brings them here to therapy. That is what brought me to therapy too."

And yet these Gods of theirs so often will not let them have this simple truth: *That we are perfectly imperfect, well meaning, ever progressing human beings, doing in any given moment the very best we know how.*

And finally it occurred to me: "I am a very nice guy, and I couldn't possibly be nicer than God."

Please think about it.

THE MOON

The moon is full once in a while. It has that ability.

And it can be many other sizes, depending on where it rests in relation to the earth and the sun.

Romantic humans tend to enjoy the moon regardless of its size or shape. We have unconditional acceptance for the moon. We don't even criticize the moon when it doesn't show up at all on a cloudy night.

The moon is constantly changing from our perspective — moving through natural cycles. That is, it is constantly changing in relation to the earth and the sun.

The actual moon is always full. The moon is never really a sliver. And half moons and crescent moons are illusions for us to enjoy.

The moon has the ability to show its fullness to us, and yet we don't expect it always.

Sometimes I wonder why we don't treat ourselves with the same love and acceptance that we have for the moon.

WISDOM AND ABUSE

Any piece of wisdom
is whole,
Always ready to be discovered.

But, if I attempt to force
my wisdom on you,
it becomes judgement...

And that is abuse.

FAMILY LESSONS

Where did you go to school? What did you learn there? What did you *not* learn there? And what did you *mis*-learn there?

Families are our almamaters, the schools we attended to learn how to be the people we are today. No matter how separate we like to think of ourselves from the families from which we first learned, any of us beyond adolescence have recognized our parents in our own actions, words, and thoughts. I remember the shock that ran through my body years ago when I heard myself telling my stepdaughters (in a loud authoritarian voice) that "beds were not made to be jumped on" — knowing perfectly well (my childhood memories intact) that beds were made for exactly that.

I have long contended that our parents, on a certain night that only parents know about, stole into our rooms as we lay sleeping and implanted in our precious little brains time capsules designed to release the essence of them (our parents) when we turned 28. If we were to have children of our own before the age of 28, the capsules would be triggered automatically within the first year of our parenthood. What a system!

Another theory: As children we are wide open, especially to our parents and other family members. Instinctively we want *and need* to trust them. We faithfully record the messages— the "family lessons" — like a hungry blank tape. We record spoken and unspoken messages alike. The silent messages are especially powerful and easily remain hidden in our adult lives as we never actually heard anyone speak the message.

Sometime between early childhood and adulthood (the timing seems to vary greatly) we *re-record* the family lessons in our own voice. Same script. New voice. My voice. And your voice.

And so when a client walks into my office, sits down and begins to berate him/herself, frequently without awareness of the self-abuse, and I ask "Who is telling you all of these mean things about yourself?", the answer usually comes: "I am."

The experience that follows is intended to help you to become more consciously aware of specifically what was taught and learned at your almamater and hopefully to encourage you in creating some additional blank tape for new lessons of your choice. But first I want to delineate an area of potential resistance and confusion about family-of-origin focus and offer a way around that potential obstacle.

IMPERFECT FAMILIES

Here is an abbreviated history lesson. First we accepted alcoholism as a disease. Then we noticed that it was hell to be in a family with a drinking alcoholic. Then we expanded our awareness to recognize other addictive disorders (other chemical addictions, gambling, food, sex, relationships, spending, etc.) Then we noticed that it was hell to be in those families too. Now the Adult Children of Alcoholics (ACOA) movement has given way to the more expansive concept of adult children of dysfunctional families. Meaning: We are products of learning centers (our families) that turn out to be far from perfect.

Granted, the preceding paragraph is highly simplified history. The point is this: We do not have to judge our families of origin as *either* functional *or* dysfunctional. The gift of expanded awareness, open-mindedness and taking responsibility for ourselves is that we can view the quality of our "family education" along a continuum. At one end of that continuum: Highly effective lessons. The opposite end: Totally erroneous, even destructive lessons. Consider that very few of us grew up in families that consistently held to either extreme of this continuum.

There are any number of approaches for taking stock of family lessons. Most psychotherapies revolve around one approach or another for becoming aware of and/or changing these lessons or belief systems. Certainly, an accurate inventory of what we learned, did not learn and mis-learned in our families of origin is central to our becoming more conscious human beings.

So for the time being, for the sake of the following exercises, let go of either/or judgement and consider yourself not a product of function or dysfunction, but a product of imperfect family lessons.

EXERCISE(S)

Here are three different approaches for taking inventory of your family lessons. Use what is helpful. Mix and match.

1) Who taught what
Make a list of significant adult family members in your childhood. Include any adults who come to mind when you recall your family, whether or not they were blood relatives. These were your teachers, for better or worse, directly and indirectly. After making your list, review each name one at a time. Close your eyes and visualize (or just think of) that person as he/she appeared to you when you were a child. In your mind, use the name for that person that you used as a

child. Tuning into each of these childhood relationships, write down what you learned from that person. Consider what you learned about yourself from how that person treated you. Consider also what you learned from how they treated themselves and other family members. What did you learn from what they said? What did you learn from what they did, or did not do? As with the previous exercises, whatever comes to mind is just right . . . so *just write it down.*

2) What you learned about what

Money. Spirituality. Feelings. Particular feelings like anger, guilt and shame. Happiness. Work. Being a man. Being a woman. Being a friend. Being a spouse. Deservingness. Giving. Receiving. Sex. Being a parent. Being a son or daughter. Alcohol. Religion. Love. Talk. Family. Fun.

Consider these categories and whatever else springs to your mind. Consider areas of your life in which you experience confusion, rigidity, relationship conflict or any other form of discomfort. List the categories or life-issues that most concern you *now* in your adult life. Take each category from your list, hold it quietly in your mind for a few minutes. Then write down what your family curriculum taught about that particular subject.

For many of us, lessons about issues that are problematic today were either grossly mistaught or not taught at all in our families. Where we need wisdom we discover bullshit or empty space. In either case, it can be very helpful to recognize that the current dilemma is not due to inherent inadequacy or character flaws, but instead results from the less-than-accurate (or adequate) educations we received from our almamater families.

Empty space, by the way is easier to fill than bullshit is to clean out. But both can be done.

3) What you decided when

There are certain times in our lives, perhaps certain life events, that precipitate psychological land-mark decisions. These decisions greatly impact *who we will become, what we will do,* and *how we will perceive ourselves* in relation to the rest of the world. Sometimes these decisions are quite conscious. Sometimes not.

Draw a life-line — just a straight line across a sheet of paper with the left end of the line (marked zero) representing the beginning of your life and the opposite end being your present age, today.

Take a good look at your life in this overly-simplified form. Mark on the line the age you were when you first left your family to live away from home. Look particularly at that space on the line between zero and your leaving home age.

Tune into your conscious memory and your gut level intuition. As you focus on this space on your life line, let your pen mark places (and indicate ages if you recall) where/when you made any milestone decisions. Don't worry about perfect recall with this exercise. Allow experimentation in your response. Write down the decisions you remember.

Many of us, witnessing the dysfunction in our less-than-perfect families will make life-affecting decisions at early ages such as:

Anger is violent. I must never be angry.
> or

I must never show my anger.
> or

Anger hurts peoples' feelings. I must never express my anger directly.

I will never act/be like my father.
> or

I will be just like my father.
> or

I *am* just like my father. (This may be a sense of affirmation or resignation.)

It doesn't pay to be emotionally honest, so I'll tell people what they want to hear.

Life is a no-win proposition, so I will give up.

I will never let them keep me down. I'll succeed beyond all expectations and really show them.

I'll be responsible for it all. If you want a job done right. . . .

I'll never treat my kids — or my spouse— like this.

POCKET QUESTIONS

Try any or all of these three exercises. Share your experience with others. And most importantly, the next time you experience conflict or discomfort in your life, reach into your pocket and pull out these questions:

> *What* did my almamater teach me about this _____?
> (subject, situation, feeling, etc.)
> *Who* taught me about how to handle this?
> AND
> *How* do I choose to live my life today?

Once the truth of your family curriculum is consciously known to you, you can go back to school —— enroll in the University of Free Choice (UFC) where every applicant is accepted.

REDEFINITION

1) *Write your family-of-origin's (spoken or unspoken)
   definition for the following words:*

Anger	*Child*	*Relationship*
Strength	*Needy*	*Weakness*
Adult	*Fun*	*Responsibility*
Love	*Family*	*Happiness*

2) *Think of some more words (important to you) for the
   list and write more family-of-origin definitions.*

3) *Choose some or all of the words on your vocabulary
   list and **write a brand-new definition** for them.
   Your choice!*

FAIR NOTICE

So, you have begun to wake up. You are becoming a conscious participant in your important life. You may even be considering the previously taboo possibility of taking charge of your own life.

You are about to make changes in the way you treat yourself, and this consequently means that you will be behaving differently in the important relationships in your life.

You have been an actor in the same play, reading the same lines, acting the same way for a lot of years. And now you are about to start improvising!

What about the other actors? What about your husband or wife or children or parents or friends or employers or employees who will still be working from the old script? What will happen when you stop being predictable?

Too often these fears, this sense of responsibility to the "status quo", interfere with our otherwise genuine desire to change and grow. So, for our own sake, as well as for the sake of others, it is important that we demonstrate respect for those we love, care about, or simply have to put up with.

Put your world on notice. Tell the people in your life that you are changing. Without having to share your personal details, and without having to justify yourself, try this: Simply tell your spouse or boss or whoever that you are experimenting with new ways of relating. Tell them specifically (as far as you know) the changes you are planning to try in relating to them, and ask for their support. Don't be addicted to getting their support, but ask for it.

Then you have done what you can do. You have been fair and honest.

Now, read from you brand-new script. Better still — improvise!

THE SHOULD-MONSTER

We are not alone. Embedded deep within many of us lives a well intentioned yet misguided parent creature we will call the "should-monster". This is the source of the inner-tyranny that has ruled many of our adult lives. Sound familiar yet?

Each of our should-monsters have their own unique style — as each have been uniquely created from our personal experience. Most often the monsters are predominately formed from our perceptions of the family in which we grew up (see "Family Lessons"). The style of any particular should-monster may be taken directly from one or both parents or may be a more original style designed especially for us (in response to parents and other external *should* givers). In either case the inner should-monster is ultimately well intentioned, believing that he/she is our protector and possessor of important down-to-earth wisdom about how this world really operates, and how we *should* go about functioning in it.

These inner-monsters are constant advice givers and especially fond of Monday morning quarterbacking, berating us with not only the "you should have this's" and "you should have that's"; but also including the "what if's...", "if only's...", not to mention the generalized criticism to keep us in our place such as: "You never can get it right" and one of its favorite attacks: "Why are you the way you are?" (Caution: Beware of the "why" questions from the should-monster. They are not really questions at all. Instead "Why" equals "You *should* be different." Listen for the implied should's in your own "why" questions.) In brief, the should-monster is the source of that pervasive guilt or shame many of us carry in our gut.

Remember: This tyranny is inwardly directed. Some of us with the most ferocious of should-monsters (mine screams at me and calls me names) are outwardly the kindest and gentlest of friends, employers, co-workers and family members. We operate with a dangerous double standard that most simply states, "You deserve a break. I don't."

Now does it sound familiar?

NEW PERSPECTIVE

Just as it is important for us to look with a more objective eye at the family lessons taught and learned years ago, it is equally essential that we gain some perspective on this inner-tyranny. Far too often, we tend to over identify with this constant critic, the should-monster, sometimes entirely losing our true identity for years and years.

To begin the process of recovery from this over identification we must become able to hear and feel the difference between the inner-part we call "should-monster" and the center-part we call (or want to call) "I".

The purpose of this exercise is to offer an opportunity to *experience yourself as separate from your should-monster.* This distinction is not automatically clear since you and your monster reside inside the same skin, and especially since one of the should-monster's favorite tactics is to deny your separateness, convincing you in fact that he/she (the monster) is who you are — certainly that you, above all, need to listen and respond appropriately to the wisdom-of-should.

Even when we experience the duality of "monster and me", we often discover that we have become "yes-people" to the almighty monster.

Monster: (Strong, powerful voice)
You are a fake. An impostor. You don't really expect any publisher in their right mind to want to publish this dribble you call a book, do you?

Me: (Meek, cowering voice)
Oh . . .I forgot. Sorry. How ridiculous of me. Of course. . . I can't do this. . . How stupid of me. . . Sorry. Sorry.

The discovery of the subservient position we take in our relationship with the monster is an essential recovery step if we are to regain the power of choice in the matter of our own self-esteem. Usually, this awareness alone will be enough to initiate change. Try it.

EXERCISE

If there is one assignment I have given to clients over the years that is more important than any of the others, this is it. Definitely share this experience with trusted friends or a group, and use it as a daily recovery tool as often as is helpful.

Two Column Journaling

Spend a few minutes alone. This time invite not only your Higher Power (and/or imagination) to join you, but also include an invitation to your should-monster. This is an exercise for increasing awareness. You will *not* need to defeat your monster in any way in order to be successful here.

Inwardly listen to the should messages. Remember that each monster is unique, and you may or may not actually hear the word "should" in the messages. Call for your monster to speak and then just listen and/or feel for the messages. A couple of cautions here: First, most should-monsters will not call themselves "monsters". They are more likely to identify themselves as conscience, inner-guide, voice of reason or a representative from God. Don't be fooled. You will recognize a should message when you hear/feel it. Second, sometimes during this exercise, one's monster is nowhere to be found. I tell my clients to beware of the monsters who wait outside in their cars when they come inside to therapy. If you call for the monster to speak and hear/feel nothing in response, that's OK. Simply rely on your memory and go on to the next part of the exercise.

Divide a piece of paper into two columns. As you listen inwardly write your monster messages in the left hand column. Write them as they are addressed to you from your monster, using your name before each message.

Monster Messages

Thom, you should work harder.
Thom, you are a fake. It's a joke to
      think you can write a book.
Thom, you'll always be depressed like
      your Mom. Give it up.

(Notice that in these criticisms most of the should's are implied.)

The most important element in writing these critical messages is to write them as they are being said *to you about you* as opposed to writing them as your personal beliefs about yourself. (i.e., I should work harder. I think I'm a fake, etc.) In this way, you begin to break out of the over identification with the monster and interrupt the "brainwashing" technique that has successfully disrupted your right to inner-peace for all of these years.

56

After completing a list of monster messages in the left hand column, go back and read them aloud to yourself. Enter your written responses to each message in the right hand column of your paper. Label this column "me", or "my responses."

I suggest that you respond in two ways to each critical message:

1) *Your opinion*: This is your thought about whether you agree or disagree with the message. It is all right if you find yourself agreeing with some or all of the messages. Keep in mind that it is your increasing awareness that will ultimately set you free.

2) *Your feeling*: This is your emotional response to the message. Avoid recording additional opinions here; simply write feeling words such as shame, anger, sadness, frustration (anger's little cousin), hurt, fear, etc.

MONSTER MESSAGES	MY RESPONSES
Thom, you should work harder. You are lazy.	1) Opinion: Your right. I agree. 2) Feeling: Shame. Sadness.
Thom , you are a fake. It's a joke to think that you can write a book.	1) Opinion: You're wrong. I am a writer and have always been a writer in my heart. 2) Feeling: Anger. A sense of power.
Thom, you will always be depressed like your Mom. Give it up.	1) Opinion: I may always have to contend with depression but that doesn't have to defeat me. 2) Feeling: Anger. Fear.

Experiment with your two column journaling. Share what you have written with a friend or group member. Have someone read your monster messages to you and *try on* different responses. Try on a shameful, subservient response, and then a powerful, angry response to say NO to the message.

Use the two column journaling method over the course of the next week. When you become aware of inner-discomfort, sit down and tune into the critical should messages. Write them down and then write *your* responses. The worst that can happen is that you will continue to have difficulty telling the difference between you and your monster. That's OK. Be careful to not beat yourself up for beating yourself up. Just practice, share with a friend and practice some more.

The best that can happen: You will listen to what your should-monster has to say, recognize a lie when you hear one, and give it the "ole Nancy Reagan" — JUST SAY NO!

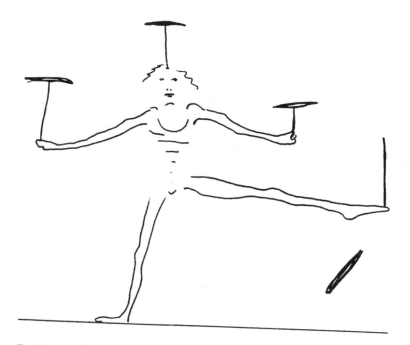

Balance and Perfection
are entirely different.

When you strive toward **perfection**
expect disappointment and self-resentment.

When you strive toward **balance,**
expect to be busy.

> **Perfection**
> *is not one of my choices*
> *today.*
> *What a relief!*

DON'T BLAME ME

Realizing that we "create our own reality" is not a way of determining once and for all who is to blame for this mess.

There is an important distinction to be made between "taking the blame" and "accepting responsibility".

Personally, I want to be responsible enough to avoid living out my life in a vat of blame.

WE'RE WRONG

*We people of low self-esteem are so **ready to be wrong.** If something negative happens within a hundred mile radius, we find a way to take the blame. "It must be me," we automatically assume.*

If we are in conflict, and I am me, and you are you, then I must be wrong . . . somehow.

*BUT . . . there is one subject about which we (people of low self-esteem) **adamantly refuse to admit that we are wrong.** That subject is our low self-worth. To this belief, that we are wrong, bad and "less-than", we hold so tightly that we couldn't possibly have space or energy for anything new — something new and radical like feeling good about ourselves.*

*The truth is we are not bad or "less-than." And we are **wrong** far less often than we previously have believed. But when it comes to this belief that we are worthless. . .*

ADMIT IT! WE'RE WRONG!

A NEW IDENTITY

We hear lots these days about discovering the child within us. This is not only descriptive of the playful, carefree elements of our personalities but also refers to a darker side of ourselves. For those of us who grew up in less-than-perfect families, the child within holds pain and cries out with needs, legitimate needs that were not met during our chronological childhoods. The child within is an emotion-filled, vulnerable part of each of us, a part that we all at one time or another attempt to hold at arm's distance, afraid of the repercussions of accepting the needs and pain as our own. In a nutshell: We find this child crying on our doorstep and haven't the faintest idea what to do with him/her.

Discovering the child-part is not difficult. Most of us have spent the majority of our adult lives feeling like twelve-year-olds (or eight-year-olds or four-year-olds, etc.) walking around in disguise, ever fearful of that dreaded day when someone would recognize that we are not adults at all — but masquerading children. This is true of reckless, irresponsible characters and super responsible stiffs alike. We tend to view others from our twelve-year-old eyes, seeing everyone else as having it all together and really being adults, while we, on the other hand, are mere impostors.

"And so," I tell my clients who have experienced the miracle of recovering their lost inner-child, "the more diffi-cult task is yet to come: Discovering the 'adult-within' ".

THE EMPTY ADULT BECOMES A PARENT

Clearly, a child within calls for a parent within. The problem that many of us face is that the nearest thing to a parental figure inside is tyrannical and full of "should's", "ought's", and other "shame on you's." (See "The Should-Monster") Most of our children within have actually been under the care and supervision of these over protective, compulsive tyrants since adolescence or early adulthood. With the rediscovery of the child within, we are challenged to recognize those old messages for what they are, and let them go — turning our attention to the creation and development of a brand-new adult; an adult who at first is quite empty, but who is destined to become the parent our child has long awaited.

"Empty" is an excellent condition when it comes time to redecorate. If you can stretch this far, celebrate your adult-emptiness. As a brand-new adult with a rediscovered child, celebrate your separateness from old dysfunctional family lessons and an outdated should-monster.

Any new parent experiences loads of fear, fear of being inadequate to the massive responsibility of protecting, loving and meeting the needs of a small human being who by definition is extremely needy. Being needy is perhaps the most natural characteristic of a child. Being fearful may be the most natural characteristic of the human parent.

What follows is an experience to help you begin to get your footing as a new parent to your "recovered" child.

EXERCISE

The purpose here is to assist you in experiencing the adult part of yourself who is able and willing to accept the substantial responsibility for the vulnerable child within. It is not unusual in this experience to find oneself slipping into the identity of that child-part, feeling and releasing stored emotions of past years. When this happens, I encourage you to take time to do this important healing work. Allow that precious child whatever he/she needs to feel the permission that is being offered.

You may also find yourself slipping into the character of the should-monster or inner-tyrant during this exercise. If this happens, please avoid the temptation to tell yourself that you are doing the exercise wrong. Simply sit quietly until you can resume the exercise in the role of either the benevolent adult or the child-self.

Allow whatever happens to increase your awareness. Find a photograph of yourself as a child. You may want to look through many old photographs as you recontact this part of your life, but eventually decide on one photo of your child-self to use in the exercise. (If you do not have access to photographs of your childhood — or if none exist — draw a simple picture to represent your child-self.)

Put the photograph in a special and safe place in your home. You may even choose to frame your picture. Treat it well. Now, for the next ten days, once per day, go to this place and sit with your photograph; sit with your child.

If you do discover that you are slipping out of your adult-self and into your child-identity during these meditations, remember that this is just as it needs to be. The only guideline offered here is to experiment with feeling the identity of *both* the child and the adult-selves. Learn to distinguish one from the other. Remember: *Multiplicity is our nature.*

For the first five days of this meditation, remain silent. Breathe deeply and gently, and use your outer and inner senses to increase awareness of this "relationship within."

Beginning with the sixth day, sit quietly to make contact with your child-self, and then begin to speak to him/her. Speak aloud even if this seems awkward or silly. Speak directly *to* the child in the present tense. And speak as an adult to a child. It may take some practice to learn to remain in your adult-self as you do so. Or it may take some practice to learn to experience the child as a reality.

When you slip into the child-self, simply notice the difference and feel what you feel. For the sake of this specific exercise, however, before you resume speaking return to the adult-self. Say whatever is in your heart.

This, by the way, is an excellent exercise to incorporate journaling. If you do so, I suggest that you not write during your meditation (time with your child) but immediately following.

If you wish to take this exercise one step further, try this: After the ten days of meditation and speaking with your child via the photograph, ask a very trusted friend to sit with you — maybe even in your special meditation place. Ask this friend to play the part of your child-self, sitting quietly with you, perhaps allowing you to hold his/her hand or even to hold him/her as you would your child.

Just as you have in your previous meditations, sit quietly for a time making contact (this time with your friend as your child-self) and just as you have spoken before with the photograph, speak now to your child.

Move slowly with this. Don't rush. When you have finished speaking to your child, sit quietly again for a few minutes before moving out of your meditation space with your friend. Reconnect now with your friend — as your friend. Replace your child-self into your heart where he/she belongs.

Finally, ask your friend to tell you what it felt like to be with you in this role, and especially what it felt like to hear and receive your words and your touch. Before you converse about the experience, really listen to what your friend has to say. This is a special gift, and is valuable feedback for your new adult-self.

A BRAND-NEW YOU

If you are at all like me, you may discover that the adult part of you who has spent the past ten days speaking to your child-self feels quite unfamiliar. This is not your mother, or your father, or your inner should-monster. This is a new part of you. With this experience you have planted a magical seed. To water and nurture this seed, we all need to practice. This is a daily practice of being a quality parent to a beautiful, deserving child.

This can be the beginning of a beautiful relationship.

THE UNICYCLE

Have you ever attempted to ride a unicycle?

*Well, it ain't easy. But as with so many skills, those who can ride a unicycle certainly make it **look easy**. Maybe this is because once the skill is learned, it is performed with ease.*

*The same is true of the skill we call "living-in-the-moment". Present tense living requires the same balance, the same focus and the same **relaxed awareness** as riding a unicycle.*

Leaning too far backward (past tense living) or too far forward (future tense living) will always result in your falling off.

Being centered on the unicycle and holding a focus on where you are going will get you there. And as long as you hold your balance, you can always change directions.

*When you are riding a unicycle or when you are living-in-the-moment, **you will be doing it with ease**. There is no other way. This feeling of "ease" is how you know you are performing the skill. Tension will throw you off balance.*

Important note:

In learning to ride a unicycle, one becomes willing to fall, even to accept bumps, bruises and scrapes. And one remains committed to standing back up, picking up the unicycle and getting back on. That's what it takes.

Happy cycling!

MEASURING RECOVERY

Measure your recovery
in units of willingness
instead of willpower,

With degree of self-acceptance
rather than self-change.

CONVERSATIONS TO CONVEY

Once at a conference for Adult Children of Alcoholics somewhere in South Carolina I heard a woman offer, as a part of her presentation, the best definition for the word "intimacy" that I have ever come across. I wish I could remember the speaker's name to give her credit, not only because I am including it here, but also because I quote her wonderful definition at least once a week in my client work. (Thank you whoever you are.)

Her definition, she told us, was simply to divide the word into syllables and read it aloud slowly.

"Intimacy" is In/to/me/see.

How safe does that feel to you? How many people in your day to day life do you trust enough to want them to "in-to-you-see"? And especially, is there one particular person in your life with whom you really want to share this treasure called intimacy?

If intimacy is your goal, then try this for the next one week of your life:

Practice Conversations
to convey
rather than *to convince.*

Read it again. Think about it. Consider a condition that plagues most all primary relationships at one time or another. The condition is "Addiction to Agreement". We are so afraid of being perceived as wrong, bad or even just imperfect by our spouses, partners, etc., that when a conflict arises, we immediately turn the conversation over to the "attorney-within" who proceeds to argue our case without much investment in having a two way communication. The goal is *to convince...* to be right. Resolution equals agreement.

"I absolutely must *convince* you to see thing my way. If you won't agree, I'll go into withdrawal! I am an agreement-junkie! Can't you see what you are doing to me!"— we unconsciously scream. And the arguments escalate into verbal, emotional and sometimes physical destructiveness — or one or both of us realizes how useless it is to continue, and we end the conversation (if that's what you want to call it) with no agreement and no one really having heard what the other had to say. Yuk.

When we decide to take a break from these recurrent, ineffective efforts to communicate and practice the art of *conversation to convey*, a giant leap is taken toward the intimacy we seek.

We emphasize taking turns in our conversations, sharing a common goal that we both have a chance to be heard. When we speak we describe what we feel as well as what we think— and we do so without attempts to convince anyone of anything. When we lose our place and slip back into old patterns of convincing, we slow down and start again.

We are simply telling the truth (as we understand it in that moment) *about ourselves.* Not how our partner should perceive the truth, and not God's ultimate truth, but just *our* truth as we are experiencing it. And we listen with curiosity and an open mind when it is not our turn to talk.

The goal of these conversations is *conveyance*. We can punctuate the communication when we each feel satisfied that what we have shared has been heard. Agreement is irrelevant here. When there are practical issues that insist on problem solving communication culminating in agreement or compromise, keep those conversations separate from the experiment of *conversation-to-convey*. Another time, another place.

It will not be easy. Expect to experience "withdrawal" symptoms as you let go of your craving for agreement. The pay off can be well worth the pain. If you meet with some success in this first week of practice, stick with it and before long you will experience . . . in-to-me-see.

Have I convinced you?

WINNING AND LOSING

*When we fight **against**
someone or something,
We lose.*

*When we fight **for** ourselves,
We win.*

SICK LETTER

Sometime when you are extremely upset with someone, and you are feeling "stuck" in relationship to that person, try this: Sit down and write the sickest, most dysfunctional letter you can possibly imagine to that person. Make a commitment to yourself not to send the letter. Just write it. Allow the most unhealthy part of you to speak through the letter. Sign it. Reread it. Read it to a friend you deeply trust.

Now: Write a second letter to the same person with the same commitment not to mail it. Allow this second letter to write itself. In other words, don't think too much about what you want to write. Let it flow out of your pen without hesitation. Again: Write it, reread it, and share it with your trusted friend.

Then: See and feel whatever happens next.

EMOTIONAL FLOW

We tend to trust our physical bodies, at least to some extent. For instance, we seldom (if ever) question the natural flow of our digestive system. We eat. We drink. We digest. We excrete. We urinate. Hopefully, we repeat this vital, natural cycle for entire lifetimes without much conscious thought, and without *critical interference* from our own minds.

[As you read this, if you have an eating disorder, you may notice that this is not entirely true for you; that you do experience critical interference in regard to your digestive system. I invite you to proceed with this analogy anyway and apply what follows to your physical digestive system as well as your system of emotional flow.]

We share the common understanding that our digestive system is a *one way track.* To reverse the direction of this system, to block the flow, even to hurry the system (unnecessary use of laxatives) is unnatural. For the sake of this discussion, let's agree that we share this healthy respect for our physical digestive process.

As human beings we are physical. Respect for that physical-ness is essential to having health-on-earth. We are also emotional, mental and spiritual beings. We tend, as a culture, to have respect for our mental-ness to the point of worship; we tend to compartmentalize our spiritual nature when we even acknowledge it; and we tend to *abuse* our emotional-ness. This abuse most often takes the form of attempts to block and/or reverse the flow of our natural emotional digestive system.

EMOTIONAL FLOW VS. CONSTIPATION

Here is a highly simplified, yet pertinent psychology lesson. Just as we ingest food physically, we live in a world of external experience, constantly taking in (ingesting) that experience. Though we do not question our right (and the necessity) of relieving ourselves by regularly using the restroom, we are constantly questioning our right to allow ourselves natural expression of our emotional responses to "ingesting" experience. If I feel the need to urinate, I do not find myself lost in inner-dialogue asking, "Have I really taken in enough fluid to justify this need? Do I really *deserve* to use the restroom?" Such inner-dialogue, of course, sounds ridiculous, and would be a needless use of my valuable mental energy. We do, however, seem to waste plenty of that valuable mental energy questioning our right to express feelings, and even our right to *have* feelings in the first place. The result, quite simply, is an emotional constipation — a build up of years and years of unexpressed emotional responses to living in a world of external experience.

The problem of this emotional constipation is compounded with the fact that after a while, these unexpressed, stored emotions are no longer easily associated with specific events from our past. We lose the ability to connect one feeling with one experience. And with that, we all too often tell ourselves that unless we can mentally make that precious connection, we had better *not* express ourselves. Since we live in a society that attaches emotional expression to blame, we helplessly abide by an erroneous law of life that dictates: "If I do not have a justifiable target for my emotional release, I had better keep my feelings to myself."

78

We find ourselves lost to the legalistic thinking that in order to have, admit to and express a feeling (especially the feeling we call anger) we must prove beyond all reasonable doubt that we have been unfairly victimized. In our efforts to be responsible we wisely want to avoid the mindset of victimization, and we are left holding the emotional bag. Unfortunately we hold this "emotional bag" *inside* our bodies where it can do the most damage.

Helplessly constipated. We live in a world of experience. We cannot help but "ingest" that experience. And yet, our options for release of and relief from this natural energy called emotion are dramatically limited by our own ineffective belief systems.

A COMMON AND REASONABLE OBJECTION

"No, no, no. . .you don't want *me* to uncork this constipated reservoir of emotion. Once I started, there would be no stopping me. . .and besides people could get hurt."

It is interesting to note that for those of us who have experienced or are experiencing emotional constipation, the blocking, swallowing, minimizing and denying of feelings was at one time in our lives the wisest choice to make. We can give ourselves credit. And it seems reasonable that now, as we consider letting go of our need to control the flow of natural emotion, we will be very frightened by the prospect of releasing what seems dangerous to us. Let's face it: If we are experiencing emotional constipation, it is highly unlikely that we have had teachers in our lives who modeled for us healthy, appropriate expression of feelings. We will be lacking lots of "how-to's."

Teaching the "how-to's" is beyond the scope of this chapter and this exercise, but we can become freshly motivated to seek new teachers (therapists, support groups, workshops, etc.) of feeling expression if we are willing to believe that there is such a thing as expressing our feelings without hurting ourselves or others. A first step in that direction is tuning into our own constipated feelings, and experimenting with releasing them.

EXERCISE

This can be an interesting and even fun exercise to do with a group, although it may seem more risky when others witness our emotional release. Even the most emotionally constipated among us have experiences of release when alone, or "blow-ups" with family members. It is a bold step we take past our shame messages when we allow someone(s) *outside of our closed family system* to really meet and greet our turbulent emotional selves.

This exercise has three parts. I will describe the experience for group work. If you are working alone, I again suggest that you at least share this experience with someone you trust.

1) **Emotional X-Ray.** Separate from the group for a few minutes. Find a quiet place to sit, breathing deeply and gently, tuning into your emotional stuckness or constipation. You may have a particular emotion in mind, or you may just follow your intuition to lead you to a constipated spot. Remain particularly aware of your physical body — you will most likely feel the blocked emotion there first. (i.e., a knot in the stomach, a constriction at the throat, tightness in the center of the chest, sensation in the arms or legs, a headache, etc.)

Once you locate the constipation, remain in quiet meditation with it for a minute or two more. Do not attempt to alter the stuckness; simply experience it. Imagine that you can see it in your body. See it, feel it, even hear it if it speaks or makes sound. Trust your imagination and intuition. You cannot do this exercise wrong.

Now use a sheet of paper and some markers or crayons to draw a picture of your experience of the constipated emotion. Draw whatever comes to mind. If you are unsure how to start, simply draw a picture of your body with the stuck emotion(s) in it. *Use your non-dominant hand to draw the picture.* That is, if you are right handed, use your left hand and vice versa. This will allow you to let go of any artistic perfectionism that you have and it will actually help access a closer connection to the feeling part of yourself — a more child-like part.

2) **Show and Release.** Returning to the group, take turns showing your art to the others. Show your picture silently first, allowing everyone to look closely at your picture and at you, the constipated artist. The silence may feel quite uncomfortable, but stick it out. It is important for us to experience sharing emotional content with each other without having to attach lots of mental explanation. This kind of communication will be brand-new to most, and may well feel very incomplete. That's OK.

After everyone has had a chance to look at one another's pictures, it is time to take another risk. Tune back into the emotional stuckness in your body. Breathe directly to that place in your physical body as if you could actually surround the stuck emotion with fresh clean air. Allow the energy of that emotion to begin to move with your breath. Open yourself and let that emotion make sound. Allow — even invite — an emotional sound to come from you. Once in touch with your sound, amplify it. *Release* the stored emotion *with the sound.* You may feel a need to physically move while you are doing this. It may help to stand up. The only rule is don't hurt yourself. Release the emotion with sound and movement. Push past blocks that will arise in the form of embarrassment and/or cynicism ("I really look silly to these people" or "This is the dumbest thing I've ever heard of.") Experience the energy movement of emotion. Release without having to offer explanation.

By the way, if this feels too embarrassing to do individually in front of a group, the group may decide, after silently sharing the pictures to use sound and movement to release the stored emotions all at once everyone participating simultaneously. Think about it — I told you this exercise could be fun.

3) **Commitment to Emotional Permission.** Finally, take a moment and write (somewhere on your picture) *an affirmation of permission,* a message to yourself granting permission to release old emotional pain. Write the most powerful commitment you are willing to make to yourself. Keep your picture and your permission message where you can see it for the next week or so. You may want to take another emotional X-Ray after a few days to chart any change or more emotional charge that needs release.

It's time that we remember that we have a right to feel. It is as natural as. . . . .

PRACTICE

Practice *identifying emotions*
and we practice **willingness.**

Practice *accepting emotions*
and we practice **self-realization.**

Practice *releasing emotions,*
and we practice **forgiveness.**

Forgiveness
is not something we do.

It is our natural state when
we are not holding onto old pain.

A GUARANTEE

Each day
practice
accepting
exactly who you are

and

You will never stop changing.

THE ANATOMY
OF CONFUSION

Have you ever been confused?

We have a tendency to include "confusion" into the category called "feelings" — as in emotions — such as anger, joy, shame, fear, serenity, guilt. Actually *confusion* is a highly effective means of *avoiding emotion*. As long as I remain confused, I will not have to identify or express my deepest feelings (usually anger, fear or shame).

"Being confused" is a versatile tool, handy also for avoiding decisions. As long as I am confused I do not have to commit to and/or take responsibility for a plan of action.

"Being confused" is a direct result of our culture's *myth of singularity*: We are supposed to be so singularly minded that we have only one opinion and one feeling at a time, and that there is only one "right" answer to each dilemma we face.

We are multiple in nature (see "A New Definition for Sanity") and when we deny this multiplicity, we block the flow of our naturally fluid, ever changing identity and remain stranded on the outskirts of self-awareness in the land of confusion.

Consider a new definition for confusion. To do so, we will use a multilayered view of self: Physical, Emotional, Mental and Spiritual.

NEW DEFINITION FOR "CONFUSION"

Spiritually — A sense of interference or disconnection in the lines of communication with Higher Power.

Mentally — More than one opinion experienced simultaneously that we believe are contradictory. (We tell ourselves that these so called contradictory opinions cannot or are not supposed to co-exist.)

Emotionally — More than one emotion experienced simultaneously that our "mind" tells us are contradictory (i.e., anger and guilt) . . . or an emotion that we experience as unacceptable or illogical.

Physically — Specific physical sensations such as tension in a particular part of the body, "butterflies" in the stomach, low or high energy, etc.

Utilizing this definition (which is, of course, only one of many ways of defining confusion) it seems that confusion originates at the mental level. The problem, however, is not multiple opinions co-existing, but a belief system that dictates that the multiplicity is unacceptable. This belief system shuts down essential "brain storming" sessions at the mental level with which we could become more fully aware of all of our thoughts about any particular subject or dilemma. The stifling belief system then slows down (or shuts down) emotional experience with "should" and "should not" messages about our feeling responses. Energy is diverted from *experiencing* our feelings to *critiquing* our feelings.

We have the physical experience (tension, jitters, whatever) of confusion as a direct result of emotions being blocked and unexpressed.

The communication lines to Higher Power are cut by the same defensive belief system so that we will not receive the message of total permission that is inevitable from our spiritual-source. Messages of total permission are not trusted by such defensive belief systems.

As is true of any defensive belief system, this seemingly paranoid procedure of cutting off contact to the outside (in the form of blocking spiritual permission messages and discouraging connection with understanding, accepting friends) and instigating tight controls inwardly (in the form of "should messages") at one time served a valuable function. However, when we begin to feel the pain of being stuck in our confusion, this particular defensive tactic has outlived its usefulness. It's time to discover the world of clear, expanded self-awareness, beyond the murkiness we call confusion.

EXERCISE

Do you ever find yourself approaching a problem in your life as if there is going to be an answer in the back of the book to prove you right or wrong at grading time?

Well, what if there isn't an answer in the back of the book? What if there is no grading time? What if there is no book!?!

This experience is intended to help bypass fear and shame based beliefs that you are not thinking "right" or feeling "right". Practice any part or all of this exercise to learn to step around that confusion inducing defensive belief system described previously, and step from the land of confusion into expanded self-awareness.

From Confusion to Expanded Awareness

Before beginning this exercise, wait for confusion to set in. If you are like me, you won't have to wait long. In a quiet place take some time to tune into yourself at each of the four levels described previously: Physical, Emotional, Mental and Spiritual. Take your time, and become an observer of yourself at each of these levels. Any judgments or critiques of your performance during this exercise are just a part of the constant flow of thoughts at your mental level. Notice them and let them pass.

Having meditated in this way, on four separate sheets of paper (one for each level) describe your awareness. Don't worry about being particularly articulate or artistic. Allow your intuition to lead the way as you characterize awareness of yourself at each of these levels.

Describe physical sensations. Draw pictures if you like. List *all* emotions you felt. Describe your emotional sensations. When you get to your mental level page, as quickly as you can write, list all of the thoughts you observed. Many of us need extra paper for this one. And finally, draw and/or write a description of you at the level of spirit.

On a fifth sheet of paper write the following statement. Use this sheet as your cover page:

"All that is described and listed here exists within me.
THERE IS ROOM FOR IT ALL . . . AND MORE!"

By the way, you don't have to *believe* what you have written on this fifth page. Just write it and keep it with the other four pages.

Commitment To Do Nothing

Review your descriptive pages of self-awareness. Share them with a friend or group. Make a commitment to yourself to do nothing about this so called "confusion" for a designated amount of time. You decide the amount of time — 24 hours, one or two weeks, six months, etc. During that time, review your awareness frequently. Add to it if you like, but take nothing away.

MANY ANSWERS (A FINAL AFFIRMATION)

I am not so much confused as I am *more* than I have habitually thought. The expanded version of me is not attached to answers in the back of the book, has a multitude of feeling responses to any given experience, and remains connected to spirit at all times.

The expanded, self-aware me knows that for every "single" question, there are *many answers*.

I am not confused. I am just right in the middle of my experience.

I HAVE A RIGHT

*I have a right
to make decisions
for myself
based on
what I want.*

*What I want
is perfectly
honorable
even though
I don't know what that is.*

VISITORS

I am not my thoughts. My thoughts are like visitors who come to call on me. Sometimes they knock. Sometimes they just barge in —usually a whole gang of them.

I am in charge here. This is where I live. And I can decide what kind of relationship **I want** with these visitors I call my thoughts.

GENERIC ADDICTION

I am an alcoholic. By the Grace of God and other recovering addicts I am alive and well today. For this I am eternally grateful. Along my recovery path, however, I have discovered that alcohol and other mood altering chemicals are not my only addictions.

I am a relationship addict, a workaholic, a control addict, a negativity junkie, as well as possessing tendencies toward food, spending, money and a multitude of other addictions. I am a "white-hat addict", severely addicted to being seen as a "good guy" by all who know me. I am battling *perfectionism* as I write this very sentence. Is this chapter perfect so far? Should I have put that last sentence there?

After a while I became tired of discovering and listing my various addictions and addictive tendencies. I began to recognize that I am quite simply an addict — *a generic addict* with the necessary talent and predisposition to become addicted to just about anything.

For me this does not negate the fact that I have a primary disease called alcoholism from which I am recovering one day at a time. Instead, the awareness of "generic addiction" enables me to expand my knowledge and practice of addiction recovery to the rest of my life. I can see that the nature of my addictiveness is to reach out to people, places, things and substances in an effort to fill my emptiness and cover my pain. I can see that this earthly reaching out became second nature to me when self-denial messages taught in my childhood (and in our culture in general) blocked what is "first nature" — unconditional spiritual love.

DEFINING ADDICTION

As nearly as I can tell, "addiction" is an accurate description of the human condition: Looking for fulfillment in all the wrong places. Combine this misdirected seeking with a tendency (even compulsion) to return again and again to proven ineffective behaviors and relationships and you have "addiction". Most simply, when I return to any perceived source of fulfillment or comfort again and again in spite of a history of negative consequences with that source, I am in an addictive cycle. Breaking out of the cycle and returning to my spiritual source is the struggle of my human-ness. I am challenged to *recover* the memory of who I am at my spiritual core. In order to do so, I must fully acknowledge my earthly addictive-ness and accept responsibility for correcting misdirected seeking behaviors that are harming myself and/or others.

POSITIVE INTENT AND FORGIVENESS

This can sound pretty heavy and frightening if you are right in the middle of battling addiction in your life. Beware of the dangerous tendency to use this information to attack yourself.

There is nothing wrong with what you or I want. Never has been. Never will be. We want fulfillment and comfort. We want to feel connected and safe. We want self-esteem. Of course we do. We need self-esteem as much as we need breakfast, lunch and dinner. And when we are hungry, it makes perfectly good sense that we seek nourishment in places (and faces) that are familiar to us.

So I can let myself off the hook — and you can too — when the "should-monster" comes to call telling me how bad I am, and how selfish I am to want anything beyond basic survival. I only want what is natural for me to want: to feel safe, loved and happy. That's all.

SELF-DENIAL: THE SET UP FOR ADDICTION

Embedded deep within our culture and expressed more blatantly through families are messages of self-denial. Self-denial messages take many forms, but ultimately they all say the same thing: The way to be loved, the way to have self-esteem is to give away our share of God's allowance. *Love equals sacrifice.*

No wonder we feel so tired, depressed or angry. We are taught to fuel everything and everyone else except ourselves. We are told to give and not to receive. We are taught this because it is thought to be right — to be the best we can do.

It is these self-denial messages taught in our early years (see "Family Lessons") that originally and continually block our source of unconditional spiritual love. When we are thus disconnected from our share of pure God (in the form of unconditional affirmation: I am wonderful and welcome just because I am me...), we naturally set out seeking affirmation, validation, temporary escape and comfort from whatever sources are available to us. These sources are relationships, chemicals, food, sex, work, money, and on and on. In short, not being equipped with a direct hook-up to an unconditional spirituality, we seek that connection on the earthly plane in the form of other people, places, situations, events and sub-stances. On the earth plane nothing is truly unconditional, and sooner or later there is a price to pay. Price or no price, we still need our fulfillment and we are *hooked*.

THE PARADOXICAL DOORWAY

So, what to do? What I did for years and years, and what most talented generic addicts do is to try, try again...keep on keeping on...never say die...all the while, dying. Our natural, desperate tendency is to work like hell to regain control when we feel that control slipping away. When we are experiencing adverse consequences that are outweighing the potential benefits of our behavior, we automatically tighten our grip and rededicate ourselves to "keeping it all together." This reflex is completely logical **and** absolutely won't work.

A paradoxical problem calls for a paradoxical solution. That solution begins with what Alcoholics Anonymous calls the "first step": We admit that we are powerless over our addiction, completely without power to control anything about our relationship with our addictive person, situation or substance. We give up our attempts to "keep it all together." And we take a giant step through a doorway toward the unconditional spiritual love we have been missing all along.

> **The paradoxical problem:**
> We are losing control and attempts
> to regain that control
> only increase the loss of control.
> **The paradoxical doorway:**
> To regain power in our lives
> we admit that we are powerless.

THE RESOLUTION

As I divest energy from my attempts to control the uncontrollable, that energy is automatically re-invested in me. My awareness of pain and emptiness increases. So as I begin to get better, I feel worse. Another paradox.

My improved connection with what is missing in me serves to encourage my sense of dissatisfaction. My dissatisfaction becomes potent motivation as long as I do whatever it takes *not* to reinvest energy back into old addictive patterns. I use this fuel (dissatisfaction) to reach "up" toward my spirit connection. I seek and find others who are doing the same, and I spend time with them. I listen carefully inwardly and outwardly, for messages of unconditional spiritual love, and when I hear them I practice believing them, but *not* giving myself away to the source of the message.

My emptiness begins to fill. My pain begins to fade.

And so the resolution of generic addiction begins. We blast through the barrier of self-denial that has stood between us and spirit for too long. We practice daily abstinence and/or balance with our identified earthly addictions. We seek support from other recovering addicts so that we can remain willing and able to fully experience our pain and emptiness as we move closer and closer to our very center. We realize that no emptiness and no pain can kill us. Only isolation can kill. And one day at a time we remain *connected.*

Connection is the resolution of addiction.

A WORKSHOP HANDOUT

Before there was this book, there was a workshop I conducted every so often at a local hospital. Once, a participant told me that it couldn't really be a "workshop" unless I offered a handout. In response to her comment I developed a handout called *Six Simple Truths*.

Now I have a "real workshop" with a "real handout" that became the first draft — the seed — for this book.

Thank you to the workshop participant who enlightened me about handouts, and my thanks to you, the reader, for having participated in this printed version of my workshop. Here is your copy of the handout:

SIX SIMPLE TRUTHS
For a Vital Self-Image

1) *I create my own reality.* The key word in this much overworked phrase is "create". From what I have been handed, I creatively build a reality for myself. "I create my own reality" is not another way to say that I am to blame for this whole mess, but instead, that I have the power to do something with it.

2) *I feel what I feel.* Once I recognize a feeling (emotion) inside, my only choice is about how I will express that feeling. Laborious attempts to talk myself out of, or in any way to try

to change or deny the feeling will simply drain me of energy that might be more effectively used elsewhere.

3) *My One-Self contains many Selves.* We are all on a path of integration. Before I can be one, I must make peace with the many. Making peace does not necessarily mean agreeing with or over-identifying with any one of my "parts". Instead it simply means that I respect those "parts" as real and valid — that I give myself permission to have more than one opinion and more than one feeling about things.

4) *My emotional-self and my thinking-self are intended for a 50-50 partnership.* An important human task is to bring this mind/heart relationship into balance, letting go of the need for one having to control the other.

5) *I am here to learn.* I let my earth life be an education. With this belief I am finally free to be the perfectly imperfect human being that I am. I no longer have to remain stuck in all or none, right and wrong, good and bad thinking. Now I can judge myself according to my intentions, and just keep learning.

6) *Self-love is true love.* I realize now that love and sacrifice are not the same; and that the most effective way to give the gift of love to others is to accept it first for myself. I remember that there is an important distinction between "selfishness" and taking excellent care of myself.

And remember:

Practice makes . . .

Practice

RESOURCES

If any part of this book has spoken directly to you, and you are interested in further self-exploration, I encourage you to reach out for qualified help. If you are in touch with your pain or dissatisfaction, know this: *Not one of us on a recovery path today has been able to do it alone.* We need each other. Fellow seekers are our primary resource. And reaching out, asking for help, is an essential part of our new definition for strength.

In seeking professional help, look for therapists who themselves have been in therapy. Find a guide who not only knows the maps, but who has been in the jungle . . . and who is not afraid to talk about the experience.

There are plenty of good self-help books on the market. Certainly no shortage there. But specifically, if you have felt a connection with *Simple Truth*, I suggest that you find a book or two on the subject of codependency and see where that takes you.

Know also that there is a growing community of recovery support groups beginning with Alcoholics Anonymous, and including Adult Children of Alcoholics, Codependency Anonymous, Alanon, Sexaholics Anonymous, Overeaters Anonymous, Smokers Anonymous, Narcotics Anonymous and more. All of these support groups are based on AA's Twelve Steps of Recovery and offer the invaluable opportunity for us to break free of our isolation and rejoin the human race one day at a time.

The human race needs *all* of us right now. It's as simple as that.

About The Author

Thom Rutledge, LCSW is a psychotherapist, author and humorist living and working in Nashville, Tennessee. Thom's second book, *IF I WERE THEY*, is what he calls "even simpler truth," blending practical self help with a unique sense of humor to create a little gift book that has been characterized as "self-helpful entertainment."

For a free catalog of Thom's books and tapes, or to inquire about workshops or speaking availability, contact his offices at the address or phone number below.

THOM RUTLEDGE PUBLISHING
331 22ND AVENUE NORTH, SUITE ONE
NASHVILLE, TN 37203
(615) 327-3423

"Be excellent to yourselves."
Bill and Ted

(from *Bill and Ted's Excellent Adventure*)

NOTES

NOTES

NOTES

NOTES

NOTES

NOTES

NOTES

NOTES

NOTES

NOTES

NOTES